OFFICIAL

FORTNITE

THE ESSENTIAL GUIDE

CONTENTS

ALL YOU NEED TO MASTER BATTLE ROYALE

Full of fun and adventure, the Fortnite Island can nevertheless be a dangerous place for the unwary. As you and 99 others face off in your quest for a precious Victory Royale, there are many strategies, tactics, and techniques that are essential to know to achieve your goal. Don't sweat it, though, because you're about to discover all the info you need right here—so you too can master Battle Royale in style.

GETTING STARTED

THE ESSENTIALS FOR SUCCESS

So you're ready to drop from the Battle Bus? Before you dive in by yourself, with a friend, or your squad, do you know what your survival strategy will be? Fortnite is a game that's constantly evolving, with new weapons, items, and themes arriving all the time, but the core aim of the game remains to be the last person standing in a Battle Royale fight to the finish. While there's a lot to be said for choosing your landing spot and simply dealing with whatever comes your way, you should also get familiar with some key "dos and don'ts" to help you secure success. This *Official Fortnite Essential Guide* reveals the vital knowledge you need for victory and takes you on a journey to becoming better in battle. So let's begin by getting the lowdown on the basics.

TAKE CONTROL

You may be quite comfortable with Fortnite's pre-set control setup, but whether you play on a console, PC, or mobile device, have a play with the individual settings to see what works best for you.

The pre-set functions include Combat Pro, Builder Pro, Quick Build, and Old School. Each one favors a certain style, allowing you to focus more on combat situations or building in a particular way. Old School lets you experience what the setup was like back in the very beginning of Fortnite.

GET TO GRIPS

Gameplay in Fortnite can be fast paced, so knowing your control options and configurations is very important. There's no right or wrong way to set up, so spend some time trying different options—asking friends what they like to have at their fingertips is also a wise move.

A RETROSPECTIVE EXTRA

The Replays function available on certain platforms lets you watch your recent matches. It can be easily accessed through the Careers tab.

TAKE AIM

Aim Assist is a helpful setting, particularly for new players. It's an option that aids you in setting sights on a target and therefore makes you more clinical in combat. Adjusting the mouse or controller sensitivity and selecting Auto Pick Up Weapons and Auto Sort Consumables to Right can boost your effectiveness too, if it suits.

PLATFORM PLAY

It doesn't matter if you're on Xbox and your friends are on PC, PlayStation, or Nintendo Switch, because you can still party up and play in the same game as them. Thanks to Fortnite's cross-platform play, you can squad up and bring your range of battle skills together in your quest to be the best on the Island.

FRIENDLY FORTNITE

Fortnite takes great pride in making the best experience possible for the huge community it has. Sharing your Battle Royale adventures with friends is really easy. You can create a friends list by sending invites to your pals. The ability to accept friend requests can be set to on or off.

ACCOUNT PROTECTION

Having a secure Epic Games account is essential. Never share your account details with anyone and keep your password safe. Enabling Two-Factor Authentication (also known as 2FA or 2-step verification) helps prevent unauthorized account access.

9

BATTLE PASS

One way to obtain V-Bucks and in-game cosmetics is by purchasing the current Season's Battle Pass. By completing Quests, you'll gain experience (XP) that'll get you to new Battle Pass levels, each one granting Battle Stars which can be used to redeem rewards. There's a new Battle Pass full of fresh, exciting rewards each Season. The Fortnite Crew subscription offer includes the Battle Pass too.

COMMUNITY RULES

The most important part of the game is to have fun and treat visitors to the Island kindly and fairly. Community Rules are in place to respect every Fortnite player. People from all around the world play Fortnite, creating an amazing community. If you feel rules have been broken and want to report a player, you can do so in-game with the Report Player option.

HAVE A HOUSEPARTY

Through the Houseparty app, you have the ability to video chat in-game with your Fortnite friends. Available to players on PC, PlayStation 5 and PlayStation 4, Houseparty needs to be open on an iOS or Android device to connect to Fortnite. When linked to your Epic Games account, you can then see the video chat on your console or computer screen.

CHANGING SEASONS

Chapter 1 of Fortnite had Season 1 through to Season X, before Chapter 2 began with a new Island very different to what had come before. Each Season delivers a new theme, storyline, and events, so while the aim is to always battle for a Victory Royale, the landscape, tests, and challenges in front of you will constantly evolve as time goes on.

HIT THE GROUND RUNNING

BE PREPARED AS YOU DESCEND TO THE ISLAND

Dropping from the Battle Bus takes just a matter of seconds, but knowing what you'll do for the first few minutes once your boots touch the ground can make all the difference in Fortnite. Here's a speedy run-through of important actions to take the moment you hit the deck. Though remember: the more time on the Island you rack up, the more your movements will become second nature.

Always have an idea of what the terrain will be like in your landing spot. More built-up places give you chance to pick up vital loot, but remember that lots of others will be thinking exactly the same. If you drop into a popular and crowded spot, the race is on to find a weapon and protect yourself.

MAKE FOR MATS

Harvesting materials (mats) is crucial. At the start of a non-Team Rumble match, you have zero Wood, Stone, and Metal, so grab your Harvesting Tool (more commonly called "Pickaxe") and start collecting these important resources. Strike at the Weak Point on the object you're hitting to harvest more efficiently.

IMPORTANT ITEMS

Discovering Chests inside buildings and all around locations gives you the chance to stock up on the valuable weapons and healing items that are contained within. Boost your Health bar by using a Medkit if you can. Ditch lower-rarity weapons for higher-rarity ones too, if possible.

KEEP TALKING

If you're playing in Duos, Trios, or Squads, you're able to keep clear communication via voice chat as you reach your landing spot. You can tell your teammates where you're going, which buildings you're searching, and whether you have any weapons or Health items to share.

ESSENTIAL EXTRA

Keep an eye on what's behind and not just what's in front of you. Spin around frequently for a full view!

SURVIVAL STRATEGY

FROM THE EARLY TO THE END GAME, SURVIVING IS SUCCEEDING

Surviving in Fortnite requires a blend of skills and strengths. You need to be able to build, loot, move, and think fast. You should also take a few seconds to scan what's around, assess any danger and decide what action to take. Battle Royale styles vary from player to player, and that's a great attraction of the game, but there are some basic survival strategies that can set you on the right road to victory. Let's explore the measures and moves you can adopt to get an advantage over an opponent.

EARLY GAME ENDURANCE

CHOOSE YOUR MOMENT

Be battle-ready the moment you leave the Lobby and take flight across the Island. The Battle Bus takes a random path across the map, so choosing your drop time and location is always a strategic choice, whether you're going solo or playing with others. But remember, the first players to land have the first opportunity to grab Items.

LOOK AROUND

When you're in the air, keep scanning the skies to check who else looks likely to be dropping near to you. If you want an easier early game, move away from these folks so that you have more time to gather resources and items. The early action can be quite hectic, but if you know where others have dropped, then you're better prepared.

ESSENTIAL EXTRA

If you have them, use headphones so that you can better pick up audio cues as to who's around. Chests also make a subtle noise before being opened.

KEEP MOVING

It's a bad move to just stand still and admire the view around you. The Storm starts circling in not long after the battle begins, so your priority is to search out Chests and stock up on mats, weapons, and other items. You are also much harder to hit if you're always on the move.

TAKE COVER

You will be an easy target for opponents if you're out in the open constantly. Running across an open field, for example, is a risky decision. Move from building to building; use walls, cars, and trees as cover and keep looking around to assess any threats. A victory is rarely claimed in the first few minutes, but you can certainly lose it by making simple mistakes.

PRACTICE PLACES

You may want to keep dropping in the same few spots, depending on the route the Battle Bus takes. Having a really good knowledge of just two or three places, and practicing your early moves there, will improve your chances of making it past the early stages. You'll have a better idea where to search, how to overcome enemy run-ins, and how to progress to the mid game.

MID GAME MISSION

LOGICAL LOADOUT

You have five inventory slots in Battle Royale (in addition to your Pickaxe slot). Also known as your loadout, this is where your weapons and items are stored and can be accessed. It's very smart to keep different types of weapons, like Shotguns and Pistols, near each other in your inventory. You want to be able to quickly select the appropriate weapon for the challenge you face, so keep slots ordered and practical!

WEATHER THE STORM

Use the countdown clock on the screen to see how long you have until the Storm shrinks the safe zone further. You need to stay inside the circle (the eye of the storm) so that you don't suffer Storm damage, which can be fatal. One tactic is to stay close to the edge of the Storm in the early and mid game, so that it's difficult for opponents to attack from behind.

COMBAT CAUTION

There's no need to rush to join a skirmish, or to start an attack that's perhaps not needed. Remember, the purpose of Battle Royale is to be the final player standing and not to rack up the most eliminations. Choose your battles wisely and only use your weapon when required—a smart player is a successful player!

EXPERT LOOTING

Eliminated players instantly drop the goodies they have gathered, which can include ammo, meds, mats, and weapons. Rushing over to scoop these up may seem like a no-brainer, but you may be putting yourself in danger if another player is patiently waiting to strike. Think about whether you actually need the dropped loot if you're already well-stacked.

END GAME ESSENTIALS

HIGH POINT

As you enter the end game and the competition has dwindled along with your combat space, taking a high point can make all the difference. Getting up on a hill or a tall building means you can look down at what's going on and identify threats. If you can't find a natural high spot, then build to give yourself elevation.

LOOK AT YOUR LOADOUT

You've organized your loadout, so now is the time to get the weapons ready that you'll need in a final shootout. This can quite often involve long-range Sniper Rifles and explosives. There's probably no need to have a Shotgun at your fingertips, for example, if you'll be doing your damage at a distance from now on. Take unwanted items out of your slots.

BUILD BATTLE

It's unlikely that you'll take a Victory Royale without building with mats. Building can give you quick access to locations, create cover, and give you an elevated spot so you can precisely aim down sights. Wood, Stone, and Metal offer different levels of protection, but Metal takes longer to construct than Wood. Being able to edit builds is also a technique you should practice.

TOP TIP

If you want to concentrate on your building skills, use Creative mode to improve your structure-making ability without the pressure of battle.

SURVIVING THE STORM

BE READY TO RIDE AND SURVIVE THE SCARY CIRCLE

The map alters, Seasons change, events come and go, and new items arrive as others are vaulted. However, the ever-encroaching Storm remains a constant on the Island. Its existence means players can't camp in remote areas and avoid attacks forever—the Storm brings all competitors together and forces a frenzy of final Fortnite action in a close space. The Storm doesn't have to be feared, though. Once you learn how to live with it, you can thrive inside the circle and use your superior skills to outwit others who struggle with its envelopments. Read on to discover some super-helpful hints about this destructive force.

UNDERSTANDING THE STORM

Learning how to handle and master the Storm is one thing, but firstly you should know how it works and the damage it can cause. The Storm has up to ten phases, each with different waiting and shrinking times. Storm phases are shorter the later the match goes on and the scramble to stay within the safe zone becomes more hectic. The maximum health point (HP) damage of being in the Storm also increases from 1 to 10 as a match moves on. So, early Storm damage is much less harmful than in the end game.

MAP IT OUT

Use the map and learn how to properly understand it, to help you stay safe from Storm damage. The Storm is represented by the shaded purple area, with the safe zone (the eye of the storm) marked by the clear circle. As it moves through its phases, the Storm area grows and the safe zone shrinks.

The white line on the map shows you the quickest route to take you to the safe zone. In each match, the Storm behaves differently, but as your Fortnite experience grows, you develop a sense for detecting Storm movements.

ESSENTIAL EXTRA

Don't think that your Shield will help you in the Storm, because it ignores Shield and drains directly on your health.

SURVIVING THE STORM

TIME TO DECIDE

When the Storm shrinks for a fifth time, the damage is already at maximum and spending time inside it becomes very harmful. While you may think that you can cope with its adversity early on, it should be avoided at all costs in the mid and end game. You need a good stash of healing items if you do need to dip in and out at this stage, so that your health can be sufficiently restored.

WHEEL AWAY

More confident and accomplished Battle Royale players will be able to cover the distance in good time and stay within the safe zone as the Storm moves. If you are caught in the wrong location, perhaps as a result of a prolonged combat, then jumping in a vehicle can get you back on track. A car, for example, will whisk you to safety and stop you taking a HP hit from the Storm.

SCOUT IT OUT

Getting involved in a fight in the Storm is never a shrewd move. Not only will your health plummet, but your vision is also impaired amidst the fog. A small selection of weapons from Fortnite's weapon history, including the Storm Scout Sniper Rifle and Night Hawk, have the ability to boost your sight when inside it.

EXPLORE THE ISLAND

How well do you know your surroundings? Are you familiar with what lies in the north, south, east, and west of the map, plus all the coordinates in between? The Fortnite Island may appear like a vast landscape, but you can soon learn what each location has to offer and the hot spots and drop zones to use to your advantage. From the range of stone buildings around Chapter 2 Season 6's The Spire, to the houses and green spaces of Pleasant Park, there's a Point of Interest (POI) and named location to suit your preferred play style. After a while, you'll remember where Chest spawn locations are as you load up your inventory for the battle ahead. It's time to travel the terrain...

THE SPIRE

COORDINATES: D4
GOOD FOR: Spire Jump Boots

Taking center spot on the Island, The Spire attracted a mass of players when it appeared in Chapter 2 Season 6. Being right in the middle of the action, The Spire was not for the weak, as danger could lurk around every corner. You could pass between the many stone buildings placed around the dominating central tower, which encased the Zero Point from Chapter 2 Season 5. Trips here could be very rewarding if you collected an orb from a Spire Guard; if you placed it down you'd earn the Mythic-rarity Spire Jump Boots to really give your game a lift. The Spire was well worth a visit early game for looting or later on as you took refuge among the buildings.

JUMP BOOST

If you collected an orb, you could place it in one of the slots at The Spire to be rewarded with the magical Spire Jump Boots.

TOP SPOT

Landing high up on the tower at The Spire could be a risky move, as many others might have been tempted to do the same. You'd need to grab a weapon and loot early on.

ESSENTIAL EXTRA

The map is constantly changing, so be prepared for new locations and POIs from Season to Season.

LAZY LAKE

COORDINATES: F6
GOOD FOR: Grabbing items and loading up for Victory Royale

Located to the west of Retail Row and north of Catty Corner, Lazy Lake arrived back in Chapter 2 Season 1 following the dramatic scenes of The End event. Showcasing a stylish bunch of buildings and suburban properties, some boasting swimming pools, it's the kind of place many would like to reside in. Well, it would be if it weren't for the frequent visitors Lazy Lake attracts who show up and cause mayhem. While it's a busy place and home to more than 30 Chests, it's not overly crowded and there's always the chance to dive through the surrounding fields and trees. Watch out for the hills around the edge of Lazy Lake, as these can attract players with a long-range weapon looking for eliminations from a safe distance.

AIM FOR AMMO

The array of ammo boxes in Lazy Lake can help you stock up a strong inventory. Be thorough as you search through the houses.

USE THE WATER

The nearby lakes and rivers give you the chance to fish. Pocketing some helpful healing items, like a Flopper and Small Fry, could improve your chances of making it through to the end game.

DIRTY DOCKS

COORDINATES: H4

GOOD FOR: Picking up metal and weapons with less opposition

Found way out east, Dirty Docks has plenty of attractions, but it can be quiet early on due to its coastal position. Don't discount it as a drop point, though, because if you're looking to avoid combat and fill up on materials, particularly Metal, then Dirty Docks is a sound option. If you're feeling brave, direct your drop to the top of a crane, hope to locate a weapon, and then target the enemy below. As a quick and fun escape, try to safely drop into the water. Inside the warehouses, there are more opportunities for Chests and items, but be aware of others looking to steal a march on you. The containers are good for cover, but you may want to build over them to boost your vision. Finally, the Motorboats at Dirty Docks give you the option of cruising away down the coast.

SWIM TO WIN

Swim around the edge of the location, picking up Chests, Fishing Rods, and items from the perimeter. Look up to see if there are any incoming threats from the mainland.

PYLON POWER

Keep an eye on the pylons above Dirty Docks. Opponents may be hiding here, looking to take out players in the open.

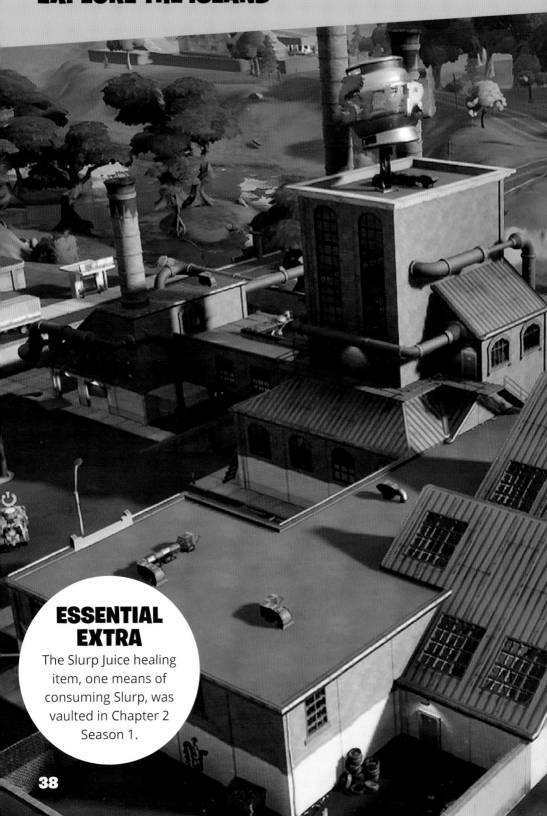

ESSENTIAL EXTRA

The Slurp Juice healing item, one means of consuming Slurp, was vaulted in Chapter 2 Season 1.

SLURPY SWAMP

COORDINATES: C6
GOOD FOR: Healing items and action among the mire

Want to make yourself feel great? A quick dash to Slurpy Swamp will soon perk you up. This location is home to the Slurp Juice factory, and the surrounding swamps and rivers were originally full of its regenerative Slurp product. Take a dip and your Health and Shield would feel the healing effects, getting you prepared to venture to nearby spots such as Weeping Woods and Holly Hedges. You could also aim for the Slurp truck and the many Slurp barrels lying around. The swamp's regen and health benefits were pretty much wiped out in a Chapter 2 Season 7 update, though, when the area became Sludgy Swamp and you could no longer get a big boost simply by wading through the wet stuff. Thankfully, Slurp barrels remained.

JUMP IN

Inside the factory, a Slurp vat will give your shield a much-needed boost. Get to know where the healing items and Chests are hidden.

FLOOD FACT

As an example of how the Island evolves, Slurpy Swamp was severely flooded during Chapter 2 Season 3 before returning to normal by the next Season.

PLEASANT PARK

COORDINATES: D2
GOOD FOR: A mix of classic combat and easy harvesting

Don't be fooled by the name, because although this may seem a tranquil and peaceful hangout, Pleasant Park can soon overwhelm you if you're not fully switched on. The open spaces in this northern location can give you a false sense of security; chances are you'll be targeted from a tree or rushed by an opponent emerging from a building. If you head here early on, search the outlying houses first for Chests and healing items and think carefully before you dash across the fields. There's a high amount of Wood to be harvested at Pleasant Park, which will be useful for building defenses and taking cover if you're caught by surprise. Pleasant Park is popular at the start of a match, and there can be heavy traffic flowing from other Points of Interest.

FIELD THE FORCE

The soccer field is a tempting place to initiate a conflict, but it's better suited to when you have safety in numbers during a Squads match.

ON THE EDGE

Land on a building's roof on the edge of Pleasant Park, then work around the outskirts if you can. Raid the attics for Chests.

ESSENTIAL EXTRA

Retail Row became
Mega Mall during
Chapter 1
Season 9.

RETAIL ROW

COORDINATES: G6
GOOD FOR: Large-scale action with a range of riches

As an original Chapter 1 Season 1 location, there has always been a lot of love for Retail Row from the Fortnite Community. Dropping here or venturing to this land of shops and houses from neighboring Lazy Lake or Dirty Docks will test your close-quarters and mid-range combat strengths. There are plenty of buildings to ransack for resources, with a medium level of Chests available. Hide behind vehicles in the parking lot or use your mats to place down temporary walls if you come under fire out on the tarmac. The buildings aren't particularly tall and getting a vantage point may have to be done by ramping. Lines of sight are pretty good, though, as Retail Row isn't too busy with structures.

CENTER SPOT

If you bring your A game, be bold and land in the center of Retail Row—it could give you the upper hand in potential engagements. Have a close- and mid-range weapon in your inventory.

SHOP TILL YOU DROP

Big Shots, Tacos, Joel's, McGuffin's, and the Noms grocery store are all part of the retail scene in this named location.

BE WEAPON WISE

HOW TO MAXIMIZE THE POWER AT YOUR FINGERTIPS

Evading the Storm, tracking the enemy, and building defenses are key skills in Battle Royale, but having an impressive grip over your weapons always remains a top priority. Without a range of weapons, you're less likely to get to the end game for a shot at a Victory Royale. This section of the *Essential Guide* serves to sharpen and hone this crucial combat craft. From knowing the hierarchy of weapon rarities to getting familiar with their core functions, you're about to discover how to get the most from these machines.

BE WEAPON WISE

COLORFUL CHOICES

As you collect weapons around the map, you'll see that they glow in a range of colors. This is because the color represents a specific rarity, and the higher the rarity, the more effective and powerful the weapon is. The five main rarities go from Common up to Legendary.

GRAY (COMMON)

Common weapons could be the first you find on the Island and will give you initial protection from enemy attacks. You'll want to swap them out for a higher-grade ASAP, though.

GREEN (UNCOMMON)

Crank up the power a notch and grab an Uncommon weapon, which improves on the damage per second (DPS) and overall damage rating. Go for green over gray if you have the choice.

BLUE (RARE)

Bag a Rare weapon and you'll see your firepower rise even more. You should always be happy to pick up a blue weapon, as your chances of breezing through the early game will increase significantly.

PURPLE (EPIC)

Now you're talking! While an Epic weapon is obviously harder to locate, you'll want to keep this by your side for the mid to end game.

ORANGE (LEGENDARY)

To operate quickly and efficiently, this weapon variation has the highest DPS and will bring you confidence when facing a fierce situation. Legendary is the way to go, for sure.

SPECIAL RARITIES

As Battle Royale changes with time, be prepared to potentially see other rarities of weapon appear. These may be for specific Seasons or tie in with a theme or storyline. For example, Chapter 2 Season 5 saw the introduction of Exotic-rarity weapons. These weapons, which included the Dragon's Breath Sniper Rifle and Shadow Tracker Pistol, could be traded with non-playable Characters using Bars you collected or earned around the map. Mythic-rarity weapons have also been a feature in Chapter 2, including Brutus' Minigun and Meowscles' Peow Peow Rifle.

BE WEAPON WISE

PERFECT PICKS

When you drop and play the early Storm circles, you should always try to seek a close-range weapon such as a Shotgun or SMG. This is because you'll be entering buildings and running into enemies close-up at first, rather than having lots of long-range fights. So, a Sniper Rifle shouldn't be a priority at this stage. Opening Chests presents a random selection of items that can include opportune weapons. Luck may or may not be with you in the weapon search, but have your eyes peeled for the perfect one to suit your stage.

MOVE SMART

Shotguns are much easier to operate when on the move, such as when you're rushing at an opponent inside a building. Other types of weapons, like an Assault Rifle or SMG, are better when you're standing still and able to focus your sights. Moving around will make you harder to hit, but it could impact on your accuracy when firing, depending on the weapon you have drawn.

PISTOL PROS

A Pistol may not match the power of a Shotgun, but this small weapon shouldn't be counted out. In Epic and Legendary varieties, its DPS is respectable and its reload speed is fast, providing a big boost during tense early shootouts. It's a starter weapon for most and combines well with another close- to mid-range option.

ESSENTIAL EXTRA

Your Harvesting Tool can be used as a close-up melee weapon, but this is very risky.

BRING THE BATTLE
THE MAIN WEAPON TYPES IN BATTLE ROYALE

SMGs

Submachine Guns, more commonly known as SMGs, are awesome for situations that need solving right in front of you. SMGs offer a high fire rate to quickly stop an opponent close up and, because they're easy to operate, your accuracy doesn't need to be that precise, either. They can burn through ammo in no time, though, so short and sharp bursts are the best and most efficient method of attack.

LEGENDARY-RARITY SUBMACHINE GUN

RARITY: Legendary
AMMO TYPE: Light
DAMAGE PER SECOND: High
MAGAZINE SIZE: High
RELOAD TIME: Medium
DAMAGE: High

The Legendary-rarity SMG is fantastic in frantic short-range shootouts and can also be used to deal significant damage to buildings and structures.

ESSENTIAL EXTRA

The Legendary-rarity Tactical SMG has a higher DPS than the Legendary-rarity SMG, but it has been in the Vault several times.

ASSAULT RIFLES

As an all-round weapon that can switch from medium- to long-range fire, the Assault Rifle is primed to help you make eliminations and survive deep into a match. If you're in a crouched position, it's a highly accurate machine with fast fire and will crumble buildings too if needed. There are a range of Assault Rifles to try out, so search for one and give it a burst to see which suits you best on the Island.

LEGENDARY-RARITY ASSAULT RIFLE

RARITY: Legendary
AMMO TYPE: Medium
DAMAGE PER SECOND: High
MAGAZINE SIZE: High
RELOAD TIME: Low
DAMAGE: Medium

The Legendary-rarity Assault Rifle definitely delivers in a match. The DPS, magazine size and swift reload time make it a mighty force by your side.

ESSENTIAL EXTRA

When available in the weapon pool, pick up the Scoped Assault Rifle to increase your accuracy even further.

SHOTGUNS

Whether in Heavy, Pump, Tactical, or Lever Action forms, Shotguns are especially useful for close-quarters combat. They pack power thanks to a good DPS, and there's no need to panic about your accuracy—just fire to deal some serious damage.

LEGENDARY-RARITY LEVER ACTION SHOTGUN

RARITY: Legendary
AMMO TYPE: Shells
DAMAGE PER SECOND: Medium
MAGAZINE SIZE: Low
RELOAD TIME: Low
DAMAGE: Medium

Along with the Lever Action Rifle, the Lever Action Shotgun showed up in Chapter 2 Season 5 to make a lasting impression. Both the Epic and Legendary variants have over 100 DPS, and players can use it in a similar way to the Pump and Tactical Shotguns.

ESSENTIAL EXTRA

Other Shotguns that have entered Battle Royale include the Charge Shotgun, Dragon's Breath Shotgun, and the Drum Shotgun.

BE WEAPON WISE

SNIPER RIFLES

These ranged weapons are the perfect choice for fights at distance, because if your aim's on point and you allow for the fact the bullet will drop slightly over a long range, you can come out on top. Use the "aiming down sights" functionality through the top mounted scope, to zone in and get your aim just right. Sniper Rifles take some getting used to, but once you have them down, your chance of victory will improve.

LEGENDARY-RARITY BOLT ACTION SNIPER RIFLE

RARITY: Legendary
AMMO TYPE: Heavy
DAMAGE PER SECOND: Medium
MAGAZINE SIZE: Low
RELOAD TIME: Medium
DAMAGE: Medium

Have only a single shot before the need to reload? With the Legendary-rarity Bolt Action Sniper Rifle, make it count and easily catch an enemy off-guard. As a tip, take a couple of seconds to be totally sure of the shot in your scope before firing.

ESSENTIAL EXTRA

Try swapping a shot from a Sniper Rifle with one from an Assault Rifle. This helps to overcome the issue of slow fire rate.

EXPLOSIVES

There's also a variety of explosive weapons in Fortnite, making a big impression when unleashed. While the Rocket Launcher is arguably the most well-known from this group, others such as the Grenade, Clinger, and Burst Quad Launcher can also deal destruction on a grand scale. When you need to stoke some shock and awe on the battleground, explosives will do the trick.

GRENADE

RARITY: Common
RELOAD TIME: Low
DAMAGE: High

Ready to have some mid-range fun? Lob a Grenade at your target and watch the explosive chaos it creates. Grenades are ideal for bringing down structures and disorientating solo and squad players. Just be careful you don't hurt yourself in the process.

ESSENTIAL EXTRA

Even though they sound similar, Grenades can't be used as ammo for the Grenade Launcher.

COMBAT READY

HOW TO TAKE CONTROL OF ~~YOUR SOLO~~ BATTLES AND MARCH TO VICTORY

If you can't control the battlefield, then there's little hope of racking up eliminations and powering through to a Victory Royale. In Solo mode, there's plenty to think about when you're on the attack and when you're under one, too. Weapon selection, function, and firing position all come into play, as well as knowing when to build, take cover, or simply run the other way. The key to combat is learning, understanding, and practicing how to respond in the scenarios you'll face. Very quickly you'll find that your reactions are second nature. Turn over to begin your combat classes.

CHOOSE YOUR BATTLES

No special prizes are given for being trigger-happy around the Island. The ultimate fighter is one who shows stealth, style, and an ability to pick the right battles. If you can avoid engaging your weapon too much in Solo mode, you'll save on valuable resources and remain focused on reaching the top ten. When the time is right to engage, the following tactics are great:

KEEP QUIET

Don't give the game away—always try to keep your noise to a minimum. In a tense combat situation where an opponent could be just around the corner, crouching and walking means you won't make loud footsteps like you would if you were running.

LOW POINT

Looking for increased accuracy with your weapon? Lower your center of gravity by crouching down and then taking a steady, targeted shot. The Assault Rifle definitely benefits from this tactic, plus you're harder to hit when you're in this position.

TRACK AND TRACE

You won't always get a warning that you're about to enter a conflict and come under attack. If bullets are suddenly zipping around you and you're caught by surprise, try to see the direction of the firing to work out where the threat is. Identifying these tracer rounds can be crucial.

BODY CHECK

Unless you have a Sniper Rifle and you're an expert at long-distance dueling, getting in a headshot is quite tricky. Instead of having to line one up and risk making no contact at all, it can be a better tactic to target an easier body shot or two to deliver swift damage to your opponent.

JUMP TO IT

It's perhaps not the smoothest of styles and can look funny, but jumping around on the Island does have some benefits. If you need to move across an open space, jumping at the same time makes you more difficult to hit if there happens to be a sniper lurking. Some weapons, such as a Shotgun, still fire fairly accurately when you're jumping up and down.

SHIELD YOURSELF

The blue bar at the bottom of your screen is crucial. If you have 100 Shield, you're in the best position to take on a combat threat and can perhaps afford to suffer some initial damage if things don't quite go your way. Getting involved in battle with a low Shield level is not a smart move.

SEARCH FOR SIGNS

Is a door open? Can you see a Chest that has already been raided? These clear clues, plus others such as buildings being destroyed and defensive forts in place, show that an enemy could well be nearby. Scan the scene for signs that an attack may be coming your way and take the early warning as your cue to prepare.

WINDOW OF OPPORTUNITY

While peeking out of a window at opponents lets you know what's going on around you, it will put you at risk. A window offers less protection than a stone or wooden wall, so decide if you really need to be nosy as it could be a costly move to make.

DISORIENTATE THE DUEL

Become a master of unpredictability! If your Solo opponent thinks he or she always has the measure of you and can predict the next move you'll make, you lose the element of surprise. Try to mix up the time you build and the time you shoot or run—keep the enemy guessing as to what you'll do next and how you behave. Remember to have a winning strategy among the apparent anarchy, though!

REAR GUARD

While building and when you have just your own eyes to rely on, don't forget to strengthen behind you as well. Your defense will be weakened if you're covered by what's in front of you but then lay yourself open to attack from behind. Place down a wall to cover you and keep swinging 180 degrees for a quick reconnaissance.

GET BETTER GRADES

Throughout Fortnite, there have been opportunities to change up your weapons by crafting, upgrading, or "sidegrading" them. Upgrade Benches, which were around from Chapter 2 Season 1 until Chapter 2 Season 4, allowed you to upgrade or sidegrade weapons in exchange for materials. In Chapter 2 Season 5, NPC Characters appeared around the Island, including Beef Boss, Kit, and Brutus, from whom weapons could be bought in exchange for Bars. Crafting, which was added in Chapter 2 Season 6, allowed you to improve a Makeshift weapon to a Primal weapon using Animal Bones. Additionally, Mechanical Parts could be used to craft a Makeshift weapon into a familiar favorite like the Pump Shotgun or Assault Rifle.

SQUAD STRATEGY

GET CLUED UP ON THE TOP TEAM TACTICS

Playing in Duos, Trios, or Squads uses the same core principles as for Solo. Now, though, you also have your pals to protect, and they can protect you in return. So Fortnite becomes a mighty team tussle packed with strategy, coordinated maneuvers, and some tough decisions. Where should you land together? How should you share weapons and items? What's the best way to handle your enemy? There are lots of advantages to squadding up in Battle Royale and making sure someone has your back. If you stick to the following team tactics and put the collective before the individual, success is sure to come your way.

ESSENTIAL EXTRA

If your friends are unavailable, you can still fill a squad with random players you don't know. Victory this way could be tougher, but just as rewarding.

TEAM TIES

The bond you have with your Fortnite teammates is what will see you through the rounds. Teamwork starts the moment you board the Battle Bus and you all decide which location to drop in. Keep chatting and land close to each other, although not too close. You want to keep a little distance so that you can form a sweep and sufficiently scout the area, collecting weapons and items and scanning the horizon for threats.

MARK IT OUT

Fortnite's ping system allows a squad to place markers on the map and the Island. This can highlight where you want to land from the Battle Bus and also display the distance you are from the marker. It's a handy tool to keep your team side-by-side and to track a specific point.

HIGHLIGHT DANGER

The marker function also lets you highlight a threat if you need to alert your squad. For example, it can help signal that an enemy player is camped out in a building. A red dot will appear and a 'Danger' sign hovers over the obstacle. It's a good tip if one of the squad is not able to communicate through voice chat.

SHOUT OUT

There's often a lot of on-screen action happening in Battle Royale. A team should let each other know the movements they are making and call out their coordinates and compass position. The compass can also be used to alert your squad to enemy positions and where incoming fire is coming from.

SPLIT UP

A squad can be highly successful in outsmarting another group of players if it can split up and form an arc around its target. This gives you the chance to cover more angles, cutting off some escape routes or hiding spots the enemy may try to use. A couple of your squad members could start with sniper shots before the others move in quickly for medium-range moves.

SQUAD STRATEGY

SHARE IT OUT

To share is to care in Battle Royale. The strength of the team is what it's all about as your squad proceeds in unison and works to keep every member operating at their highest level. Make sure each player has the key weapons, like a Shotgun and Assault Rifle, as well as a stack of mats and healing items. Drop something if you don't need it to let a teammate pick it up and get a boost. Share the workload too and cover your squad with protective fire if they venture to a danger area.

MEDS MUST

Sharing healing items like Shield Potions and Med Kits benefits the whole team. Some of your squad may be less experienced than other members and frequently take more damage, so giving them a restorative boost makes sense. The Chug Splash is a thrown healing item that revives those within its splash radius, and the Chug Cannon, which arrived in Chapter 2 Season 5, replenishes both Health and Shield.

SHAKE IT DOWN

Now you can really get to grips with rival squads! Called a Shakedown, this is when a knocked opponent can be grabbed and shaken to reveal the location of his or her nearby teammates. It's a top tactic, but be careful: During a Shakedown you can't move for a few seconds, so only use it when the coast is clear.

REBOOT REWARD

An eliminated teammate will drop a Reboot Card, which another teammate can collect and take to a Reboot Van to revive them. More than one Reboot Card can be redeemed at the same time. Watch out, though, because a respawned player has very limited resources and the Reboot Van will also sound and flash, potentially alerting opponents to your whereabouts.

ESSENTIAL EXTRA

Look for campfires across the map—they have the power to raise an entire squad's Health for 25 seconds.

KNOCK, KNOCK

Here's a tactic that could see you set a trap. If you can knock an opponent instead of eliminating them, you don't always need to rush in to finish the job. A knocked player is no threat to you. A less-than-savvy teammate of the opponent may quickly show up to revive the fallen player, giving you the chance to strike at them as well. Always scan the scene to see if others will rush in before you do.

DOUBLE UP

With a teammate by your side, you both have the chance to target an opponent and eliminate them in quicker time. Often it will make more sense for you both to focus your weapon on the same enemy player, with the outcome being a speedy takedown and one less opponent for your gang to deal with. Work together to take down your targets.

TRIPLE THREAT

The same tactics as with Duos and Squads can be applied to Trios. Here, players just have to adjust to having two friends working in tandem with you around the Island. A team of three makes for great matches in Battle Royale and you'll soon work out each other's strengths and combat qualities.

BUILD BETTER

HOW TO MAKE CONSTRUCTIVE CONSTRUCTIONS

Building is one of the main foundations of Fortnite and is essential to going deep in Battle Royale. While it is possible to do very little of it to reach the end game, you would be hindering your chances of success, as building helps you with key maneuvers such as creating cover, offering elevation, and providing access to new places. From basic single-player principles to more advanced construction in team fights, having a great grasp of the building game will get you far.

WALL

There are four main types of builds that create the basics of your constructions. First off, and most importantly, is the simple wall. Whether in Wood, Stone, or Metal, the wall is easy to place but can be a real lifesaver. If you need some quick shelter, slapping this down provides you time to respond and reload ammo. Defensive walls are usually wooden because it's the quickest material to generate.

FLOOR

Placing down a floor tile will build some helpful bridges. Floor tiles can add height and stability, plus they can get you moving where you need to be—a tower fort can have a floor and platforms bolted on to bring you to a new position of attack or defense.

STAIRS

Also known as a ramp, this building structure can only "raise" your combat ability. Stairs can be grand or basic, but however you lay them out, they give you the high ground, protection, and, if needed, an escape route. Wooden stairs are quick and simple to create but can be taken out quite easily.

ROOF

Perhaps you call it a pyramid? Whatever your term, placing a roof can be the final piece in a simple or more detailed build. Always remember to protect yourself from above, so capping off a quick 1x1 or a taller tower can stop unwanted threats from the air. Sure, not every construction needs one, but do keep this structure in mind.

BOX CLEVER

Never count out the classic 1x1 box build, consisting of four joined walls placed as you swivel with a ramp inside. From the early to the end game, you'll be surprised how often you unleash this technique. The 1x1 is cramped but the ramp gives you the opportunity to carefully peek out and fire while dropping back down for cover. When mats and time are precious, it can be a vital creation.

TO BUILD OR NOT TO BUILD?

Obviously there are plenty of towers, houses, and factories already standing around the Island, and you can choose to shelter in these and operate from a ready-made base. This is quick and saves your resources. However, running for a building will take time and could result in you suffering damage you can't afford. So although there will be a pre-existing option at times, it's not something you can rely on and you'd be wise to learn how to build by yourself to succeed.

STAY STRONG

Any build is quickly done using Wood, but this is the least protective material. In the end game, when you're not moving so much or ducking from the Storm, consider beefing up your structures with a higher-grade resource. A box, mini tower, or double ramps reinforced with Metal or Stone will need much more force to knock down and will keep you safer from attacks than their wooden counterparts. Try to make sure your material counts as close to the 999 limit as possible so that you have a ready supply at your fingertips.

GET CREATIVE

Fortnite Creative is THE place to head to if you want to spend some serious time trialing and perfecting your building skills. In its peaceful Islands, you have infinite materials and can really focus on extravagant constructions and creations. The techniques you pick up here can be used when the fight is back on in Battle Royale. Look out for special Creative Island codes, offering you access to some amazing scenes from some of the best Community builders. Take a trip to these places to pick up some inspiration for what's possible in the building game.

IMPROVE WITH EDITING

Being able to edit a building will become a helpful tool as your building ability expands. Editing means you can customize a building, adding helpful extras such as a window in a wall or an escape door to exit from. These moves can greatly boost your chance of collecting eliminations—as well as show off your construction skills! Experiment either in Battle Royale or Creative with how to make the most of this function. Remember that you can only edit your own buildings or those constructed by your team, not structures put up by opponents. Feel free to reset your edits if you're not happy with them.

ITEMS INFO

Having a reliable weapon at hand could be your route to Victory Royale. But in Fortnite, there are other clever items you can use to overcome your opponents—these may not lead directly to an elimination but could well be indispensable in your quest for success. Players must make the most of the objects they have around them, whether these are found naturally or from a Chest. From fish to forageable food, Shockwave Grenades to Harpoon Guns, keep your eyes open around the Island for these various items.

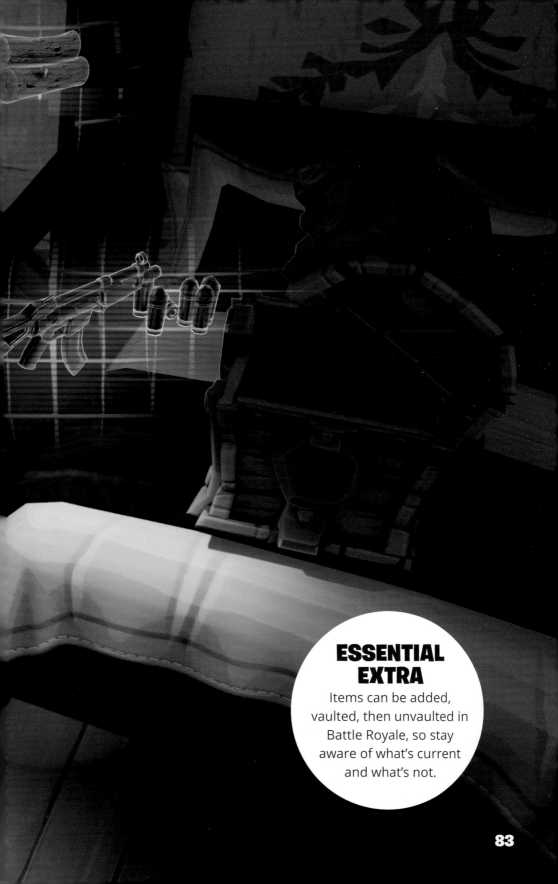

ESSENTIAL EXTRA

Items can be added, vaulted, then unvaulted in Battle Royale, so stay aware of what's current and what's not.

CAMPING OUT

Campfires can be difficult to locate, but if you find one, use it as a great way to heal yourself and your team. After you light it, the fire can revive 50 Health over 25 seconds to all nearby players—just make sure you can spare that time and won't be surprised by an approaching enemy. The campfire isn't moveable, but the healing process can be quickened by adding Wood. If you find a campfire that's already been used, adding 300 Wood will ignite it.

GO FISHING

Make time for a quick spot of fishing, which is not only fun but extremely beneficial. Casting your Fishing Rod at a fishing spot allows you to catch Health-restoring and/or Shield-restoring fish. Some fish species can provide other benefits as well, such as temporarily giving you a speed boost. If you're using a Pro Fishing Rod, you may be able to catch fish species you wouldn't be able to otherwise. Also, with any Fishing Rod, it's possible to catch weapons to add to your arsenal. You can additionally use a Fishing Rod to snare a squadmate or enemy and fling them a short distance.

WATER WONDERS

Let's look a little closer at the array of fish on offer. These range from Small Fries offering 25 Health to Floppers boasting 40 Health and Shield Fish raising your Shield by 50. A Slurpfish can increase Health or Shield, and the Thermal Fish, which showed up in Chapter 2 Season 4, had the ability to highlight enemy players once consumed. Don't forget the lethal Loot Shark, which appeared in Chapter 2 Season 3. This fearsome creature can be controlled with a Fishing Rod and steered towards an enemy before unleashing a dangerous bite.

FOOD FOR THOUGHT

Staying on the topic of healing items, foraging for food on the ground will also improve your Health bar. Forageable food may seem small and insignificant, but consuming an Apple or Corn, for example, will top up your Health by 5 and 10 HP, respectively. Forageable items can be stacked in large quantities and used when needed with just a one-second consumption time.

PULLING POWER

An incredible item with great all-round abilities, the Harpoon Gun is something to grab if you see it in Fishing Barrels, Chests, or as floor loot. It's an effective close- and mid-range weapon when fired at an enemy and has the ability to pull a player closer to you. The Harpoon Gun will also unleash significant damage to buildings when the hook makes contact. Use its 10 charges wisely because once it's used, it can't be replenished. You can also use it to go fishing for some catches at quick speed.

SUFFER FROM SHOCK

Want to cause a shock to the system? The Shockwave Grenade is not an explosive item but actually one for putting some distance between you and the place you were standing. When caught in its blast radius, you and your squad will be flung high and wide, which may help you escape a dangerous situation in an instant. You can also toss it at your enemy, but keep in mind that it does not hit Health/Shield or cause fall damage.

LAUNCH TIME

Put some distance between you and your opponent by placing a Bouncer item down. Classified as a Trap, this special piece can be attached to walls, floors, and roof surfaces, and when a player makes contact with it, they'll be flung away. A Bouncer can help you evade the Storm or chase down an enemy. When placed appropriately, they can also disrupt the plans of an opposing player, so have some fun and slap one down to deal some disruption.

ITEMS INFO

BURNING UP

Arriving in Chapter 2, the Firefly Jar is a hot little item that is capable of causing some widespread damage. Firstly, you need to spot a group of distinctive swarming Fireflies—found in waterside or forest areas—then interact with them to produce the item. The Firefly Jar can be thrown and, when it breaks, there's a chance it will set light to nearby wooden structures. It deals an instant 40 damage to opponents or buildings and then 10 more per second.

PROVE A POINT

As some items come in and out of the game, be ready to adapt to your surroundings and make the most of the objects available to you. For example, in Chapter 2 Season 5, Zero Point Crystals emerged as a method to get a teleportative boost. These items could be found in the desert around the Zero Point. After consuming one then jumping while in the air, they would propel a player forward at super speed.

GONE BUT NOT FORGOTTEN

Sometimes items return as part of a Limited Time Mode (LTM) or an event. In Chapter 2, the Balloon item was featured in the Floor Is Lava LTM, giving players the opportunity to float away to safety. The Winterfest event in 2019 saw the return of many items, like the Boogie Bomb, which makes players dance for 5 seconds if they're caught in the blast radius. Making use of older items again for even a short spell can be gratifying.

REVVED AND READY

GET BEHIND THE WHEEL AND DRIVE TO VICTORY

Back in Chapter 1 Season 4, the Shopping Cart showed up as the first vehicle for players to traverse in. Since then, the All Terrain Kart (ATK), Quadcrasher, X-4 Stormwing, and Choppa, among others, have all scrambled across the Island in one way or another. The introduction of the first drivable cars was a real game changer in Chapter 2, as they gave players the chance to get behind the wheel of a variety of automobiles. Having a sedan, sports car, pickup, or semi at your disposal obviously changes the dynamics of combat, as well as giving you a fun new way to move around the map.

ISLANDER – PREVALENT

Labeled as "the spirit of responsibility," the Islander Prevalent is a four-door family sedan that still has enough speed to safely whisk the driver and three passengers to safety. A solid all-rounder, it can cause ram damage on opponents and buildings if needed and is also quite easy to steer when compared to larger vehicles. The fact it can carry four gives it an advantage over the quicker Whiplash sports car.

VICTORY MOTORS – WHIPLASH

Built by Victory Motors, the Whiplash sports car is a faster alternative to the Prevalent. However, its higher speed is traded off against it only being able to transport two players. If you're trying to make a scene from behind the wheel, then the Whiplash is a real head-turner with precise handling. It's also the only drivable car with the option of a speed boost. Be careful, though, because the boost will drain the fuel tank.

OG – BEAR

Take yourself and three passengers on an off-road adventure. The Bear pickup is well-suited to the terrain if you need to cut across fields and dirt, and being bigger than a sedan, it's capable of much more impact damage. The two rear passengers are in a good position to scout for targets and fire at the enemy, but they also have less protection there compared to riding safely inside the Prevalent.

TITAN – MUDFLAP

A true titan of the road, the Mudflap can cause chaos with its huge size and power. This semi, made by the Titano company, is awesome at ramming and makes light work of knocking out buildings and any opponents caught in its headlights. Speed and acceleration are not the Mudflap's strong points, but if you and a teammate jump up into one, you'll still be enjoying the drive.

RIDE THE ROAD TO VICTORY

Drivable cars arrived in Chapter 2's Joy Ride update, with players getting to take to the road (or the off road) in new ways. Unlike the more straightforward Shopping Carts and ATKs, there's a little more to think about when you're behind the wheel of a sedan, sports car, pickup, or semi.

THINK OF THE FUEL

All cars need refueling at some stage. When you first sit in the driver's seat, you'll see what's currently in the tank and have an idea of the distance you can cover. When the fuel runs low, that's your cue to visit a Gas Pump or to keep an eye out for a Gas Can. You can also take a Gas Can with you to save for later.

NOISE PATROL

Each car has a vibrant engine under the hood that will kick out some noticeable noise. Be mindful as you cruise around with your crew because the sounds you create can alert nearby enemies that happen to be in earshot. Sometimes, it pays to jump out of the car ahead of the action and cover the final distance on foot in an effort to keep the peace.

TIRE TRACKS

It's possible to shoot out the tires on an opponent's vehicle and cause them to have speed and steering problems. You'll need to be a skilled shooter to hit the rims from a distance, though.

WATER WAY TO TRAVEL

Chapter 2 Season 1 made a big splash with the introduction of the Motorboat. No longer were vehicles restricted to the land and the skies, with the X-4 Stormwing having already made its mark in the air. With four seats, the Motorboat makes big waves and gets a team on the move. Another advantage of cruising the water is being able to use the Motorboat's missiles to take out opponents.

ESSENTIAL EXTRA

There are exciting changes all the time in Fortnite, so expect new land- and air-based machines to enter the game at any time.

OUTFITS GUIDE

SWITCH UP YOUR LOOK IN BATTLE ROYALE

Whether it's through a trip to the Item Shop or as part of the Battle Pass, acquiring a new Outfit is a highlight for many players. This cosmetic feature can transform your player into a huge variety of appearances, ranging from a fearsome warrior to a secret agent, robotic fighter, sporty soldier, and just about anything else you can imagine. There are hundreds of Outfits to explore, and some even come with customizable options so you can really tailor your unique look. Never be shy of catching the eye of other players!

OUTFITS GUIDE

THERE'S A STYLE TO SUIT YOU

With so many Outfits to choose from and the Item Shop being updated frequently, players have many options when it comes to changing their appearance. Express yourself in your own style... want to be an ancient warrior one day then a metallic creature the next? Sure thing!

SET IT OUT

Every Outfit is part of a Set. There could be just one Outfit in the Set, but the set can also feature other Items including Gliders, Pickaxes, and Back Blings. Looking through the Set lets you match up your look with accompanying items if that suits you. However, you may fancy switching things up with items from different Sets. Mix and match how you like!

CLASSIC LOOK

While new Outfits always catch the eye, there's also something to be said for rocking up in a classic look from the past. Characters such as Tomatohead, Cuddle Team Leader, Beef Boss, and Raven are among the favorites in the community. Look out for such beloved Outfits rotating into the Item Shop.

AWESOME OUTFITS

MANCAKE

INTRODUCED: Chapter 2 Season 5
RARITY: Epic

Unlocked through the Chapter 2 Season 5 Battle Pass, this unmistakable owner of the "Butter Barn" comes from The Breakfast Bandit Set, which also features the Flapjack Flyer Glider, Breakfast Bounty Back Bling, and other items. Mancake is part man, part pancakes, with an extra twist of the Wild West for good measure. He's also dripping in syrup and butter, making him a tasty addition to the Island.

MEOWSCLES

INTRODUCED: Chapter 2 Season 2
RARITY: Epic

This mighty, muscle-bound Outfit could be the "purrr-fect" choice when deciding your appearance for battle. Meowscles is included in the Swole Cat Set and was among the spies from Chapter 2 Season 2's Battle Pass. His machine-loving son Kit was introduced in the Chapter 2 Season 3 Battle Pass.

OUTFITS GUIDE

BRUTUS

INTRODUCED: Chapter 2 Season 2
RARITY: Epic

Chapter 2 Season 2 was stuffed with menacing Outfits, and among the top of the pile was Brutus. Like other Battle Pass Outfits from this Season, this imposing, shaven-headed spy has three bonus Styles: one of gold plus the choice of "Ghost" or "Shadow".

LEXA

INTRODUCED: Chapter 2 Season 5
RARITY: Epic

Lexa, introduced in the Chapter 2 Season 5 Battle Pass, was the first anime-like Outfit in Fortnite. She was soon joined by another anime Outfit: Orin from the Y-Labs Rescue Set.

RAVEN

INTRODUCED: Chapter 1 Season 3
RARITY: Legendary

Dark, mysterious, foreboding... Raven can be described in many ways, but he will always send shivers down your opponents' spine. When this unforgettable Outfit pops up in the Item Shop, it's well worth checking out.

FISHSTICK

INTRODUCED: Chapter 1 Season 7
RARITY: Rare

Fishstick has been popping up in the Item Shop for quite some time now, but his popularity remains as strong as ever. Partly person-like with a whole lot of fishy features mixed in, it's difficult to confuse this Outfit with any other you could come face-to-face with.

TNTINA

INTRODUCED: Chapter 2 Season 2
RARITY: Epic

Complete with her built-in Boom Emote, TNTina was another standout inclusion in the Chapter 2 Season 2 Battle Pass. She teams up perfectly with the Bombs Away! Glider and Kabag! Back Bling, both part of Short Fuse Set alongside her.

AGENT JONES

INTRODUCED: Chapter 2 Season 6
RARITY: Epic

The Chapter 2 Season 6 Battle Pass included this prominent rescuer of Reality. Agent Jones has five further Styles, which change his sophisticated look to ones much more customary for combat.

TELLING THE TRUTH

FORTNITE'S MYTHS AND MYSTERIES EXPLAINED

There is a lot of information, news, and talk online about Fortnite. Quite often, there will be an amazing claim made about something that can be done in the game or a top new tip to try, only for it to turn out to have no basis in reality. The bottom line is that you shouldn't believe everything you see or hear! Here, we'll sort the bona fide from the falsehoods and rubber stamp the reports as true or false. Let the fact-checking commence...

A PEPPER MAKES YOU SWIM FASTER!

While consuming a Pepper does give you a 60-second speed boost on dry land, it does not have the same effect when you're in the water. To go a little faster in the water, try "dolphin diving" across the surface, which is done by tapping the jump button.

FALSE!

VEHICLES CAN'T OPERATE IN WATER!

Hear us out because this is true, but also a tiny bit false! The four main types of drivable cars introduced in Chapter 2—the Islander Prevalent, Victory Motors Whiplash, OG Bear and Titano Mudflap—can survive for a very short while on the water before sinking and being destroyed.

TRUE

LARGE ROCKS OFFER MOST BRICK!

Looking to harvest Stone as quickly as possible to rocket up your resources? Instead of bashing away at a building's brick walls, look out for large grey rocks. Targeting these with your trusty Pickaxe is the most efficient way to gather Stone, which is a valuable resource in the mid and late game.

TRUE

THE CHUG CANNON DEFEATS THE STORM

That's a big no, we're afraid to tell you! No item will protect or shield you from the Storm's damage indefinitely. The Chug Cannon is a very useful healing item for a squad, but it's not invincible.

FALSE!

THE SHADOW TRACKER ACTS LIKE A SHAKEDOWN!

It sure does, which is why players enjoyed getting their hands on the Shadow Tracker when it dropped during Chapter 2 Season 5. Like a shakedown, it highlights targets for all your team to see.

TRUE

GAME MODES

Dropping on the Island and squaring up against 99 others is just one aspect of Battle Royale. Solo, Duos, Trios, and Squads have enough action and adventure to keep any level of player engaged, but there are also other exciting options to explore. Get hyped up and head to Arena to improve your competitive skills, chill out and build within your own rules in Creative (technically not part of Battle Royale, but included with it!), or jump into LTMs or Party Royale. With this variety, the fun is never-ending in Fortnite.

GAME MODES

ENTER THE ARENA

Arena focuses on getting your game ready for the competitive scene. The more you progress and the more competent you become in combat, the more Hype you'll earn, through eliminations and placements. Look to boost your Hype level to promote you to the next division and open the path to competing in events for rewards and cash prize tournaments.

GET CREATIVE

Build your own games, special structures, and unique experiences on your own Island for you and your friends to explore. Creative is all about letting your imagination escape and setting your own rules. It's the perfect place to practice your moves and the key mechanics of the game.

IT'S PARTY TIME!

Relax and enjoy the party—eliminations are out of the question in Party Royale. This is a social space to enjoy the company of other Fortnite players, with minigames all around and shows such as movies and concerts. Keep an eye on what the next show will be!

REACH THE LIMIT

Limited Time Modes (LTMs) are part of the regular Battle Royale experience. If you've never entered an LTM before, give it a go as the range of rules and aims brings a new twist to your gameplay. The Fortnite world can look a little odd here compared to what you've been used to, but in a good way!

GAME GLOSSARY

EPIC GAMES

The developer and publisher of Fortnite Battle Royale. Battle Royale was released in 2017.

PvP

This means Player vs Player. In Fortnite Battle Royale, players battle against other players for victory.

VICTORY ROYALE

If you are the last remaining player, Duo, Trio or Squad on the Island, then you take the Victory Royale. This is the ultimate goal.

BATTLE PASS

A reward system where rewards can be unlocked the further you progress in a Battle Royale Season.

V-BUCKS

Fortnite's in-game currency. V-Bucks can be used to pick up things such as Outfits, Pickaxes, and Emotes.

VAULT

Sometimes, certain weapons, healing items, and vehicles are placed in the Vault, being removed from the Island. These may leave the Vault and return to the Island in the future.

2FA

Two-Factor Authentication (2FA) is an important tool that increases security on your Epic Games account. Enabling 2FA unlocks the Boogiedown Emote as a reward.

BATTLE BUS

At the beginning of a match, players drop onto the Island from the big, blue, flying Battle Bus that moves across the map in a random direction.

STORM

The Storm draws in during each Battle Royale match and moves in a random direction. Always stay within the Storm's safe circle to protect your HP.

HUD

Head up display. The amount of information displayed on your screen during a match. Your HUD can be configured to your own preferences.

COMMUNITY

The Fortnite community is the millions of players of the game from around the world. Community discussion often happens in places like Twitter, Reddit, and Discord.

LTM

Short for Limited Time Mode. An LTM is a special sub-mode over a set period of time and has different rules to a standard Battle Royale game.

ADS

Aim down sights. A player may be able to focus their aim (aim down sights) when using a weapon to increase their accuracy.

POI

Point of interest. A place on the Island whose name shows up when looking at the map. These places often have standout buildings or features. There are many POIs, and they can change from Season to Season.

MATERIALS

Harvesting Wood, Stone, and Metal materials ("mats") gives you the resources to build and protect yourself on the Island.

SEASON

Each Fortnite Season brings a distinct theme or big changes to Battle Royale. For example, Chapter 2 Season 2 brought in spy factions and Chapter 2 Season 3 saw the Island in a submerged state.

STREAMER

A Fortnite player who broadcasts their gameplay live, letting other players watch their (often entertaining) pursuit of victory.

OUTFIT

The main component of how your Fortnite character looks. Outfits can range from dinosaur costumes to disco divas to futuristic fighters to sentient objects.

First published in the UK in 2021 by WILDFIRE
an imprint of HEADLINE PUBLISHING GROUP

Hardback 978 14722 8815 8
Written by Kevin Pettman
Design by Amazing15
All images © 2021 Epic Games, Inc.
Printed and bound in Italy by L.E.G.O. S.p.A.
Every effort has been made to fulfil requirements
with regard to reproducing copyright material. The
author and publisher will be glad to rectify any
omissions at the earliest opportunity.
Headline's policy is to use papers that are natural,
renewable and recyclable products and made from
wood grown in sustainable forests. The logging
and manufacturing processes are expected to
conform to the environmental regulations
of the country of origin.

HEADLINE PUBLISHING GROUP
An Hachette UK Company
Carmelite House
50 Victoria Embankment
London, EC4 0DZ
www.headline.co.uk www.hachette.co.uk

www.epicgames.com